A Kid's Guide to Drawing™

How to Draw
African Animals

Justin Lee

The Rosen Publishing Group's
PowerKids Press™
New York

For my sister Katie, who has helped me to appreciate the value of art

Published in 2002 by The Rosen Publishing Group, Inc.
29 East 21st Street, New York, NY 10010

First Edition

Book Design: Kim Sonsky

Layout: Michael Caroleo

Project Editor: Frances E. Ruffin

Credits: p. 6 © Index Stock; p. 8 © Brian Vikander/CORBIS; pp. 8, 12, 14, 16, 18, 20 © Digital Stock.

Lee, Justin, 1973–
      How to draw African animals / Justin Lee.—1st ed.
         p. cm.— (A kid's guide to drawing)
      Includes index.
      ISBN 0-8239-5790-X
      1. Animals in art—Juvenile literature. 2. Wildlife art—Juvenile literature. 3. Drawing—Technique—Juvenile literature. [1. Animals in art. 2. Drawing—Technique. 3. Zoology—Africa.] I. Title. II. Series.

      NC780.L35 2002
      743.6—dc21   00-012297

Manufactured in the United States of America

CONTENTS

1 Let's Draw African Animals   4
2 Addax Antelope   6
3 Dromedary Camel   8
4 Cheetah   10
5 African Elephant   12
6 Cape Zebra   14
7 White Rhinoceros   16
8 Giraffe   18
9 Male Lion   20
   Drawing Terms   22
   Glossary   23
   Index   24
   Web Sites   24

Let's Draw African Animals

Africa is the second-largest **continent** in the world. Much of Africa is desert. Deserts are very hot, dry areas in the world that have few plants and little water. The continent of Africa also has **savannas**. Many African animals live in savannas, which are huge areas of land with tall grass. Africa's animals also live in its deep forests and rivers.

People from around the world travel to Africa just to look at the animals in their **habitat**. They come to see a **pride** of lions resting in a savanna, giraffes stretching their necks to munch on leaves at the top of a tree, or a family of elephants enjoying an evening bath in a lake. Africa is home to so many special animals that huge parks have been created to protect them.

Not everyone can go to Africa, but people can get to know the animals of Africa by visiting zoos or watching movies or television shows that feature them. Another good way to learn about African animals is to draw them. You might study a giraffe's long neck or appreciate how big an elephant really is, or understand why a camel has a hump. Most of all, you will appreciate how **unique** each animal is.

Here is a list of supplies that you will need for drawing African animals:

- A sketch pad
- A number 2 pencil
- A pencil sharpener
- An eraser

All of the drawings begin with a few simple shapes including ovals, curved lines, rectangles, and triangles. To better understand these terms, turn to page 22.

Some people learn to draw faster than others do. If you are slower at learning to draw, keep practicing and drawing. Pretty soon, your sketch pad will be like an exciting piece of the savanna. Your animals might look like they can jump off the page.

Addax Antelope

The addax is an antelope that lives in the dry, sandy Sahara desert of North Africa. The Sahara usually gets less than 10 inches (25 cm) of rain a year. Desert animals must live long periods of time without drinking water. The addax gets most of its water from special plants that store water in their leaves. The addax also has **adapted** to desert life by having broad, flat **hooves**. These hooves prevent them from sinking into the soft desert sand. During the summer, the addax's fur is white. This reflects the sun and keeps the animal cool. Because of its white coat, many people call the addax the white antelope. They also have beautiful, long, **spiraled** horns.

1

Begin the addax by lightly sketching two ovals. Compare the tilt of the back leg oval to the clock face. Draw lines to connect the ovals, top and bottom.

2

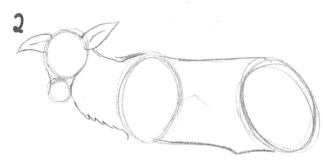

Sketch a circle for the head, centered at the top of the shoulder. Sketch a smaller circle for the nose and mouth. Add ears. Draw jagged lines to connect the head to the body.

3

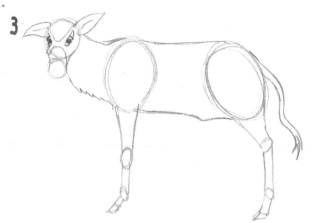

Draw the eyes. Look at the way one sits on the edge of the circle, and one doesn't. Add curved guidelines for the facial pattern. Sketch small, light circles for the leg joints. Draw the front and rear legs. Notice how the tilt of the oval shows you the angle of the top of the rear leg. Add the tail.

4

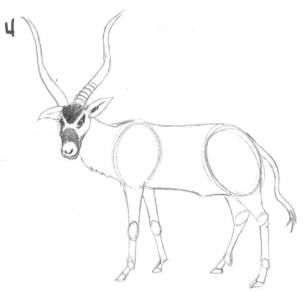

Lightly draw the graceful, spiraling horns. Then add small, curved lines for the ridges on them. Add nostrils and the mouth. Shade the darker area of the face and ear. Lightly sketch the joints and limbs of the other two legs. Note where each line intersects the overlapping lines of the body or leg.

5

Because the addax is light colored, you don't need to shade the whole body. Make lighter pencil strokes toward highlighted areas. You don't need to shade in the lightest areas. Starting with the darkest areas of the body, add light, short pencil strokes for fur. Leave the belly and side lighter.

7

Dromedary Camel

There are two kinds of camels. Dromedary camels live in North Africa. They have one hump. Bactrian camels are found in Asia. They have two humps. African dromedaries are about 6.6 feet (2 m) high at the shoulders. The dromedary camel can walk for 18 hours without stopping. It also can go for a long time without drinking water. This makes it a very good work animal. The hump on a camel's back stores fat. That fat is useful when the camel needs energy. A camel can go up to 17 days without water. On a long trip, a camel can lose a lot of weight. It gains it all back as soon as it finds water. A camel can drink up to 25 gallons (95 l) of water at once.

1

Sketch a large, slightly tilted oval. Sketch a smaller oval, off-center, for the hump. Add a vertical oval for the rear leg.

2

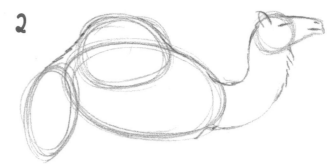

Sketch a small circle for the head at a level with the top of the hump. Add lines to form the front of the head. Draw the mouth and nostril. Add the eye and ear. Draw the gently curving (and slightly shaggy) lines for the neck.

3

Draw a calloused knee at the bottom front of the leg oval. Sketch circles for the leg joints. Add curving lines to complete the rear legs. Draw wide, almost triangular shapes for the camel's spreading hooves.

4

Next add the front legs. Notice the callus on the front of the front leg. The calloused areas on the front and rear legs are from kneeling to lie down and get up again.

5

Using your eraser, carefully clean up sketch lines you no longer need. Add pencil strokes—always in the direction of the hair and contours of the body—to shade just the shadow areas. Go over the outline with a sharpened pencil. Add a shadow beneath the camel, and (why not?) a couple of pyramids in the distance.

9

Cheetah

Cheetahs are the fastest land animals on Earth. They can run more than 60 miles per hour (96.6 km/h). These amazing animals can take steps that are 22 feet (6.7 m) apart when they are running. That would be like jumping almost three times your own height! Cheetahs live in the savannas of Africa. They have light yellow coats that are covered with black dots. This helps them hide in the grass. All cheetahs have two black stripes that run down their faces to keep the light from reflecting in their eyes. Unlike many other big cats, cheetahs hunt in the daytime. Cheetahs are **predators**. They catch and eat other animals. Cheetahs need to be fast to catch **prey** such as gazelles and rabbits.

1

Draw a small oval, almost straight up-and-down, for the shoulder. Lightly sketch another tilted oval for the body, and yet another inside it. Make a small line connecting the tops of the first two ovals.

2

Draw a tilted oval for the head. Draw two light lines to connect it to the body. Add the tail. Draw lightly!

3

Look carefully at the angles of the rear leg. The leg goes straight down from the front of the inside oval. Where is the bend, compared to the first oval? How far forward does the paw reach? Draw the rear leg.

4

Sketch the front leg, starting from the middle and the bottom of the shoulder oval. Look at the space between the legs as you draw, and notice how the front leg aligns with the rear paw.

5

On the chest and belly of the cheetah, add short pencil strokes for fur. Draw the other front leg. Draw the head, adding ears, and lines at the mouth and nose.

6

Add the triangular eye, with the cheetah's distinctive tear lines from the eye. Add bumps on the back at the shoulder and hip. Lightly erase oval lines that you no longer need. Use the tail as a warm-up for drawing spots.

7

Use short pencil strokes in the direction of the fur for shading. Take your time with shading and the spots. Sharpen your pencil. Sharpen outlines.

African Elephant

The African elephant is the largest land animal in the world. A male elephant can be 10 feet (3 m) high at the shoulders and can weigh up to 8 tons (7.3 t). Elephants live in the grasslands of Africa, below the Sahara desert. African elephants are larger than their cousins, the Asian elephants. African elephants have larger ears and trunks than their Asian cousins, and their backs are more curved. Elephants never travel far from water. They like to take baths every night. Elephants breathe through and make noises through their trunks. They use their trunks to grab leaves that are high in the trees. They only eat plants, never meat. An African elephant can eat up to 500 pounds (226.8 kg) of food per day.

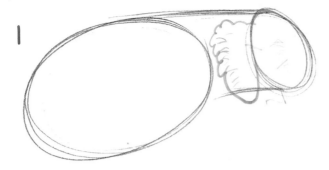

1

Before you draw, use the clock face to identify the angles of the two ovals you will draw first. Start with a large oval for the body of the elephant. Add a smaller oval for the head. Does the head oval touch the oval of the body? (It shouldn't.) How much space is between them? Lightly sketch lines to connect the body and head.

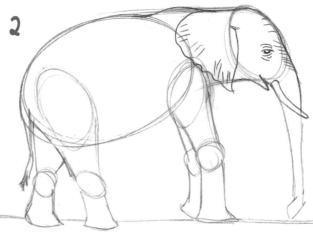

2

Look carefully at the angle of each leg. Does any leg go straight up and down? Lightly draw a line for the ground. Draw the legs, very lightly at first, using ovals for the knees, as well as the hip and shoulder. From the sides of the head oval, draw gently curving lines for the trunk, reaching almost to the ground. Where the trunk joins the head, add a tusk and the mouth. Directly above that, draw the eye. Add a bump on the top of the neck. Draw the ear and notice that it covers much of the neck.

3

First complete the outline of the body. Add a bump on the back and a small bump on the stomach. Add toenails! Go over the outline of the elephant, and carefully erase lines you don't need—for example, those ovals you started with.

4

Now begin to shade, starting with the darkest parts of the elephant. How much white do you see on the final drawing? Not much! Because the elephants are gray, your whole elephant should be gray when you finish. Look at the final drawing, or look at a photo of an elephant. Study the wrinkles in the elephant's skin. There are zillions of them! Next add lines showing the direction of the major wrinkles.

13

Cape Zebra

Zebras are beautiful animals. Everyone loves their black-and-white striped skin. Cape zebras live in the rocky mountains in Cape Province, an area in South Africa. They feed on the grass that grows in the mountains. Cape zebras grow to be almost 5 feet (1.5 m) tall at the shoulders and can weigh 850 pounds (386 kg). These animals can live for more than 25 years. They live in family herds, usually of one male and five or more females. Cape zebras like to roll in the dust to protect themselves from insects. At one time, the Cape zebra was close to **extinction.** There were fewer than 100 left in the world. Thanks to people who want to protect them, there are now about 1,200, most of which live on protected land.

1

Lightly sketch two tilted ovals. Look at the clock face to make sure you have them tilting like the example. Connect them with a curvy line for the back.

2

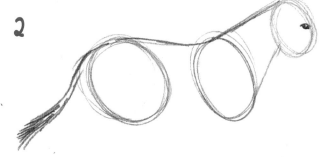

Add the tail (easy!). At the opposite end, draw a light oval for the head (again, notice the tilt of the oval). At the very front of the oval, draw the eye. Notice where it lies in relation to the shoulder (above it). Draw the two lines of the neck.

3

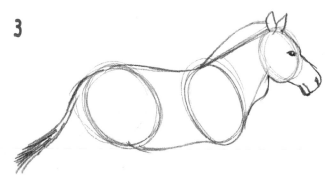

Add ears, a light outline of the mane, a bulge at the throat, and a snout, complete with nostril and mouth. Draw lightly until you're sure you have it right!

4

Lightly sketch the legs, using light ovals at each joint to help you understand how the leg bends. The rear leg bends in three places. Look at the clock face and compare angles if you find part of this confusing.

5

Ah, what a difference we see in this drawing! Add the two other legs, lightly at first, observing angles and joints carefully. Lightly erase the ovals. Although they are helpful in getting the drawing started, we don't want them to show through the stripes!

6

Add stripes and shading, and curving pencil strokes for grass.

White Rhinoceros

The white rhino is the second-largest land animal after the elephant. A full-grown white rhinoceros can be 6 feet (1.8 m) high at the shoulders, more than 13 feet (4 m) long, and weigh more than 2.5 tons (2.3 t). The white rhino lives only in Africa. Even though it is called the white rhinoceros, it has thick, gray, hairless skin. The white rhino, like the elephant, doesn't eat meat. It is a **grazer**, which means it eats grass and small plants. Rhinoceroses have very poor eyesight. Most of them can see only a short distance. They rely on their senses of smell and hearing instead of their sight. The white rhino has two hard horns on the end of its nose. If the horns are broken off in a fight, they will grow back.

1

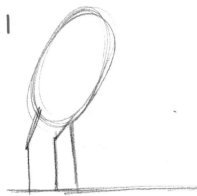

Lightly draw a tall, tilted oval for the rhino's hip. Look at the clock face to see the angle of the tilt. Add two bent lines showing the leg nearest you, and another straight line for the leg on the other side. Draw a line for the ground.

2

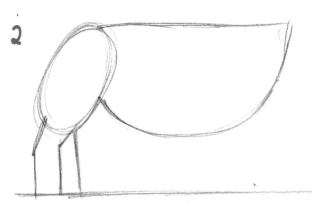

From the top of the oval, draw a horizontal line for the back, and a swooping, sagging line underneath for the belly. Extend the line for the ground.

3

From the front of the body, draw a line straight down and toward the rear legs. Under it, add the front leg closest to you, then the one behind it. Sketch the shape for the neck.

4

Draw a rectangle for the head, getting smaller toward the front. Add the two horns and the tail.

5

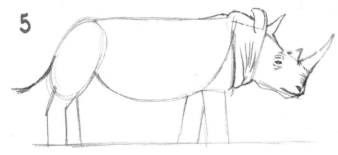

Now you'll find many details to add as you refine the head. Draw lightly at first, and observe carefully. Add the eye and arcs around it, below and behind the smaller horn. Make the front of the head bulge out slightly and add a nostril and wrinkles. Add curves to the bottom of the head and neck, and wrinkles. Draw the ears and the bulges at the top of the neck.

6

Look at this finished drawing. Add curves to the legs, widening them to make feet. Draw toenails. Draw lines for the ribs, then shade with short pencil strokes. Make the bottom of the body and the inside of the far legs darker. Follow the direction of the wrinkles as you shade the face. Add grass, and a small bird to keep the rhino company!

17

Giraffe

The giraffe is the tallest animal in the world. A giraffe's long neck has the same seven bones that we have in our necks, but their bones are much longer. A giraffe's neck alone can be taller than the average adult human, and can weigh almost 500 pounds (227 kg). Most giraffes grow to be about 17 feet (5.2 m) high. They can weigh as much as 4,215 pounds (1,912 kg). The giraffe **evolved** into such a tall animal because it uses its neck to feed on the top leaves and branches of trees. Giraffes live only in the woodlands and savannas of Africa, south of the Sahara. They have two natural predators, lions and humans. The giraffe is not an **endangered** animal. There are about 100,000 giraffes in the world.

1

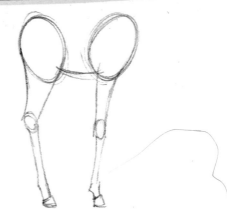

Lightly draw two ovals, tilted slightly outward. Use the clock face to help see the correct angles. Connect the ovals with a small, curved line on the bottom.

2

Draw the two legs closest to you, using small ovals at the joints. Notice how the rear leg is larger at the top, and how its angles are different from the front legs.

3

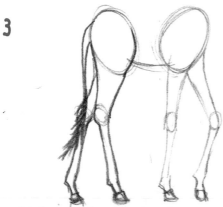

Add the two legs farther from you. Draw them lightly at first, so that you can change them if you need to—note that the length of the legs at the hooves was adjusted. Fortunately, the leg bottoms get fairly well hidden by grass in the final step! Draw the tail.

4

Make a light oval for the head, far above the body. Add the angled lines of the neck. Draw a light line for the back. Sketch the outline of the mane, ear, and horn.

5

Draw the front of the head, with nose and mouth. Make a horizontal line with a curved line below it for the eye, and draw another curved line above for the eyelid. Use short pencil strokes to create the mane. Go over the whole outline to refine it. Lightly erase the ovals and any other lines that you no longer need.

6

Note that giraffes have dark patches that are four-sided, but not square.

Male Lion

The lion lives in the savannas of southern Africa. It is called the king of beasts. Male lions can weigh up to 600 pounds (272 kg). They have huge muscles and can jump 12 feet (3.7 m) in the air. They can run up to 35 mph (56 km/h). Male lions also grow a thick **mane** of dark fur. Lions are the only big cats that live in groups. These groups are called prides. A pride has mostly females, their cubs, and only a few male lions. Male lions protect the group from other animals such as leopards and hyenas, who might try to steal baby lions for food. They also protect the pride from other male lions that try to take the females for themselves. While the male lions protect their pride, the females hunt for food.

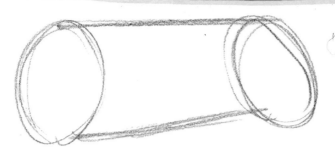

1

Draw a tilted oval for the lion's hip. Draw the shoulder oval and lines to connect the two ovals, being careful to leave enough space for the body.

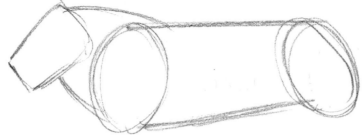

.2

Draw the boxy shape of the lion's head, slightly smaller at the mouth end. Notice the angles of the box. Add curving lines for the top and bottom of the neck. Where do they connect to the body?

3

Draw a line for the ground, and use light circles and lines to map out the legs. Pay close attention to the angles, and look at the shapes between the legs (negative space) as well as the shapes of the legs themselves. Add the nose, mouth, eye, and ear. Use short pencil strokes for the whiskers, mane, bottom of neck, and at places on the body where muscles show.

4

Continue shading, emphasizing the muscles. Leave contrast between light and dark to suggest strong light. Go over the outline, especially on the legs.

Drawing Terms

Here are some of the words and shapes that you will need to draw African Animals:

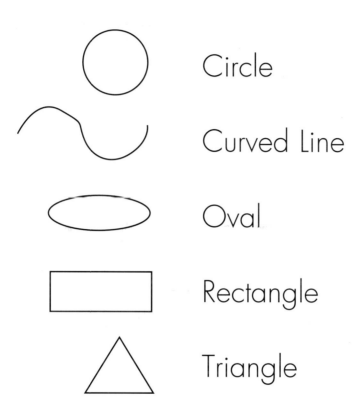

Circle

Curved Line

Oval

Rectangle

Triangle

Glossary

adapted (uh-DAPT-ed) To have changed to fit new conditions.

continent (KON-tin-ent) One of the seven great masses of land on Earth.

endangered (en-DAYN-jerd) When something is in danger of no longer existing.

evolved (ee-VOLVD) To have developed and changed over many years.

extinction (ik-STINK-shun) No longer existing.

grazer (GRAY-zer) An animal that feeds on grass.

habitat (HA-bih-tat) The surroundings where an animal or plant naturally lives.

hooves (HOOVZ) The hard, hornlike substance that covers the feet of some animals.

mane (MAYN) Long, heavy hair that grows about the neck and head.

predators (PREH-duh-ters) Animals that kill other animals for food.

prey (PRAY) An animal that is hunted by another animal for food.

pride (PRYD) A group of lions that live together.

savannas (suh-VA-nuz) Areas of grassland with few trees and bushes.

spiraled (SPY-ruhld) Having a curved or coiled design.

unique (yoo-NEEK) One of a kind.

Index

A
addax antelope, 6
African elephant, 12

B
Bactrian camels, 8

C
camels, 8
Cape Province, South
     Africa, 14
Cape zebras, 14
cheetahs, 10
continent, 4

D
desert, 4, 6, 12
dromedary camels, 8

E
elephants, 12
endangered, 18
evolved, 18
extinction, 14

G
giraffe(s), 4, 18

L
lions, 4, 20

P
predators, 10, 18
prey, 10
pride(s), 4, 20

R
rhinoceros, 16

S
Sahara, 6, 12, 18
savanna(s), 4, 5, 10,
     18, 20

W
white rhino, 16

Z
zebras, 14

Web Sites

To learn more about African Animals, check out these Web sites:
www.seaworld.org/infobook.html
www.nationalgeographic.com/